Bow Wow!:
Ohio Dogs in History, Mystery, Legend, Lore, Humor & More!

by
Carole Marsh

gallopade publishing group

Other Carole Marsh 📖 Books

OHIO JEOPARDY
OHIO FESTIVAL FUN
OHIO CATS IN HISTORY
CHRISTOPHER COLUMBUS COMES TO OHIO
OHIO SILLY TRIVIA
OHIO "JOGRAPHY"
OHIO COASTALES
OHIO QUILT
OHIO QUIZ BOWL
OHIO STATE GREATS
OHIO DISASTERS & CATASTROPHES
OHIO BANDITS, BUSHWACKERS, OUTLAWS & CROOKS
OHIO SCHOOL TRIVIA
OHIO CHRISTMAS TRIVIA
OHIO KID'S COOKBOOK
OHIO HARD-TO-BELIEVE-BUT-TRUE HISTORY & MYSTERY
OHIO PIRATE & TREASURE TRIVIA
OHIO HOT AIR BALLOON MYSTERY
BEAST OF THE OHIO BED & BREAKFAST
IF MY OHIO MAMA RAN THE WORLD
OHIO FOOTBALL MYSTERIES
OHIO BASKETBALL MYSTERIES
SEX STUFF FOR OHIO TEACHERS OF KIDS 7-17
THE BIG INSTRUCTION BOOK OF OHIO BUSINESS
OHIO LIBRARIES
OHIO BOOKSTORES
OHIO MEDIA
CHILL OUT!: OHIO MYSTERIES
OHIO CRINKUM-CRANKUM
OHIO MYSTERY VAN
OHIO MATH
OHIO GAZETTEER
OHIO KUDZU COOKBOOK
OHIO PHYSICS
OHIO EXTRATERRESTRIALS
OHIO SNOWSHOE & EARMUFF

Table of Contents

✏ A Word From the Author 4

Lick Your Chops!: Canine Cuisine 5
Patch, the Pirate Dog 6
Best-In-Show 10
A Dog's Body 12
A Breed Apart 13
Draw a Picture 15
Around the World With Dogs 16
Sex Ed, Dog Style 17
Bow Wow!: The Dog's Bark 17
Tombstone Territory 18

I Love My Ohio Dog 18

Obedience School 19
Show Off! 20
Dog History 20
Famous Dogs In History & Legend 21
Dog Talk 22
Doggone Trivia 23
Appendix 25
👓 About the Author 32
Glossary 33
Bibliography 34
☞ Index 36

BK LS

A Word From the Author

Dogs are part of our lives. From Snoopy and Ruff in our morning comic strips . . . to President Bush's Millie on the noon news . . . to reruns of Benji, RinTinTin and Lassie (interrupted with commercials about Pluto), dogs help make up our days.

I learned to read with Dick and Jane and Spot. Do we really remember such small doggie details after all these years? Well, a couple my age just opened up a hot dog stand called, "Dick and Jane's (their real names) Dog Spot"!

My childhood calendar was marked with dogs from cocker spaniels to collies. I had a St. Bernard once who thought he was a horse. I'm not kidding! We finally had to let a rancher adopt him and last I saw, he was galloping over a hillside with the rest of the steeds.

My best dog, bar none, was Bugs, an Old English sheepdog. The story in this book, "Patch, the Pirate Dog" is based on him. Bugs was the kind of dog we call "man's best friend". I liked to walk for exercise, but he would never come along, *unless* it was dusk or dark. Then, nothing could keep him from tagging along as my protector.

He liked to bring me big, fat, smelly eels from the river as presents -- and wanted me to play catch with them with him! Because he had all that shaggy hair over his eyes, he thought if he couldn't see me, I couldn't see him. So, believing he was "invisible", he would parade through the house doing things that were "No-Nos" until I whispered, "Bugs!" I'm sure he did not think that was really me talking, just his conscious bothering him enough to rush back to the kitchen where he belonged!

Bugs' favorite thing was to ride in the back of a convertible or in the bow of a boat. Both let the wind blow his hair away from his eyes so he could see the big wide world.

Kids can learn about the big wide world just by reading about dogs. See if you don't agree!--cm

Lick Your Chops: Canine Cuisine

No longer do dog-owners just throw out any old bone. Here are just a few of the tasty new tidbits your hound can chow down on!

- **Gourmet Treats:** cookies in the shapes of lollipops, goldfish, nachos, English crumpets and bagels.

- **Bo's Bone:** an all-natural bone-shaped cookie you can share with your dog.

- Bone-shaped cookies in gingerbread, oatmeal, peanut butter and carob chip flavors.

- Tasty Morsels with Chlorophyll & Yogurt Drops

- Dog food in ribbon-wrapped jars and gold packages

- Food with diaries for newborn puppies; food with bow tie necklaces with dog bone charms inside.

- Diet dog food

- Pasta for dogs

There are also now chefs who cook for dogs on yachts. Some restaurants are even serving meals to dogs. One Ohio parent complained that she could buy healthier food for her dogs than for her children! Many dogs are now vegetarians (like their owners). If you were a dog, what food would you like to eat?

And now here's a story about a special food dog!

Patch, the Pirate Dog

It all started in a little waterfront 🏙️ town in Ohio. I had this great dog named Bugs. No, he wasn't named for creepy-crawlies. His real name was *Bugati* and he was named after a northern Italian restaurant I loved because they had all these super deserts piled high with whipped cream and filled with lemony pudding drizzled with chocolate. (Is your mouth watering yet?) But we called him Bugs for short.

Bugs was an 𝕰𝖓𝖌𝖑𝖎𝖘𝖍 𝖘𝖍𝖊𝖊𝖕𝖉𝖔𝖌. Now I know you're picturing one of those Walt Disney movie sheepdogs all clean and white and fluffy with that cute pink tongue hanging down. Bugs had the pink tongue and his eyes were completely hidden behind thick bangs, but he was seldom clean and fluffy. I tried, but Bugs loved to run and play and roll and jump in 〰️ water -- dirty or clean and then shake all over you, of course.

Bugs had a job. It was unofficial, but he was the Welcome Dog, sort of like the Welcome Wagon. When anyone came to town, Bugs walked them up one side of the waterfront and down the other. He never got tired of this. He escorted everybody: old folks; little kids; moms with 👶 baby carriages; boaters. He was so popular that people all over talked about him. We were proud of Bugs and ♥ loved him a lot.

Then one day a terrible thing happened to Bugs. Really *two* terrible things. A 🚗 hit-and-run driver ran over Bug's left leg with the front tires of a car . . . and the back tires threw up a board that hit Bugs in his 👁 right eye.

As you can imagine, we rushed our pet to the vet's office as fast as we could. The 🩹 doctor just shook his head, but told us to leave Bugs and go home; it would take a while for him to see what he could do, if anything.

We were *sooooooooo* sad. Everyone in town called to wish Bugs well. People walked up and down the waterfront with sad faces because there was no Bugs to escort them around 🚦 town.

Finally, the vet ☎ called. We held our breath to hear the news. "You can come and get Bugs now," he said. We raced back to the vet's office, afraid of what we would find. The vet seemed very serious. Then he opened the office door and let us into the room. There was Bugs! He wagged that lump that passes for an 𝔈𝔫𝔤𝔩𝔦𝔰𝔥 𝔰𝔥𝔢𝔢𝔭𝔡𝔬𝔤'𝔰 tail for all he was worth.

But we froze in our 👣 footsteps. We were shocked! For the vet had done two things to Bugs. Over the eye Bugs had lost, he had tied a *black patch*. And on the end of the leg that he'd had to amputate (cut off), he had put a *wooden leg* with a gold-looking tip on the end. "Bugs," I said, running to hug him. *"You're a pirate!"* ⛵

In a few days, Bugs was back on the ▦ streets of our small town. I guess because his hair had always covered his eyes, he didn't mind the patch at all. It took him a while to get used to the wooden leg (even though many dogs get around just fine with three legs). But soon he was strutting around town like he was something ☆ special.

One day Bugs was escorting a 👤 new man in town up the street. When they got to the end of the block, the man patted Bugs and said, "Thanks for the company, Patch." And so after that day, Bugs had a new name -- *Patch the Pirate Dog*.

🛑 Later that day, the man came running back down the street. He was very upset. "What's wrong?" someone asked him.

"Something terrible has happened," he said. "I am moving here soon to buy a new 🏠 home, get married and open a new business. I brought all my money with me in a leather 💼 case. But now it's gone!"

The police were called. The neighbors looked. Everyone looked ^{high} and _{low,} _{low} and ^{high}. There was no leather case to be found, full or empty. The poor man was more upset than ever. Everywhere the man went, Patch went too. But 🌙 night came and it looked like all the man's dreams were to come to a very sudden and sad end.

Now I forgot to tell you one thing about Bugs, oops, I mean Patch. He was *nosy*. He liked to stick his cold, wet nose into everybody's business. I used to tell him he was going to get that nose caught in a 🧀 mousetrap one day if he didn't look out. But that dog didn't pay any attention, he just kept on poking around. This meant that I often found some pretty weird things on my doorstep in the mornings after he had prowled around all night. And this morning was no exception, for there on the top step was a plump leather case with a very weary-looking 𝔈𝔫𝔤𝔩𝔦𝔰𝔥 𝔰𝔥𝔢𝔢𝔭𝔡𝔬𝔤 guarding it.

"Patch!" I said, "You're a hero!" And he was! As soon as the man and the town heard that Patch had recovered the man's money, they came by to shake his paw and give him a pat. But Patch just acted like Patch and escaped all the petting so he could walk some more folks up and down the waterfront.

Patch had recovered from his accident. The man had left to get his wife-to-be. Things were quiet in town. Then one day Patch got a ✉ letter in the mail. A big, fat letter. I picked it up at the post office. Everyone was standing around when I opened it for Patch. I read the note to him:

Dear Patch,

I've been wondering how I can suitably reward you for recovering that leather case. For you not only got all my money back, you did much more. You got my dreams back. Like you, I had a bad mishap with a car a few years ago. It took me a long time to recover and to earn enough money to get married, buy a home and start my own business.

I had one idea for a business, but have now changed my mind. My wife and I plan to open The Ohio Dog Biscuit Company in your town. I would like to offer you the job of Chief Taster. If you want the job, please put your pawprint at the bottom of this letter and return it to me.

But before you decide, perhaps you'd better try the product you will be testing.

At that point, I dumped the rest of the contents of the letter on the floor. If there is such a thing as dog booty, this was it. For there on the floor were six dog biscuits -- each in the shape of a pirate doubloon or piece-of-eight! In just a moment, there were *none*. It appeared that Patch, the Pirate Dog wanted the job!

And you know, I think the man got a bargain, because Patch also doubled as night security. But on his lunch hour (since he was stuffed and didn't need to eat anyway!), Patch still

escorted newcomers up and down the waterfront: 👓 old folks, little kids, moms with baby carriages, and especially the ⚓ boaters. Many of the boaters even waited for him and when they saw him coming threw up their hands and cried, "Avast, Patch! We'd best not set sail without giving you a pat and a hug for good ☘ luck!"

Every now and then, just for good measure, when Patch and I are alone, I whisper to him: *"Bugs?"* What does he do? He licks my cheek with that wet, pink tongue and then he barks roughly. "Ok, ok!" I say. It's clear this dog likes being Patch and I make it a point never to argue with a pirate -- even a four, I mean *three*-legged one! ☺

✉ One Ohio dog puts his "nose-iness" to good use. He stands by the table while his master addresses letters. When he gets the stamps out, the dog licks his nose and his master touches the stamp to it then sticks in on the letter! The dog then licks his nose to get ready for the next stamp.

🐕 Best in Show?

What are the 10 most popular breeds of dogs in Ohio? According to the American Kennel Club:

cocker spaniel   Labrador retriever   poodle
golden retriever   Rottweiler   German shepherd
chow chow   dachshund   beagle   miniature schnauzer

What breed was the underdog? The mutt, of course!

One Ohio dog likes to start the morning with a cup of coffee, just like its owner. The vet says one cup is ok -- in fact, add a dash of cream!

Dogs can get sunburned, so keep them inside in the middle of the hottest summer days. Also, dogs can swim, but they may not be able to get out of a swimming pool or a strong water current, so keep an eye on them!

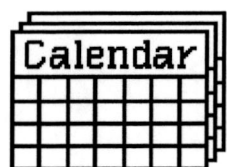
September is Share Your Love for Dogs Month!

30% of Ohio dog owners celebrate their dog's birthday!

There are over 54 million dogs in the U. S.

Ever wonder what your dog is up to when you leave home? Use your camcorder to find out!

The American Rescue Dog Association (ARDA) was founded in 1972. It provides search and rescue dogs for emergencies free of charge. The dogs must be double-coated, agile, and smart, and they must have a good smelling ability without showing any hunting instinct. Their handlers must be fast-thinkers and good decision makers; they must be strong, patient, and smart about all kinds of things from first aid to how people lost in the outdoors would behave. Sound like tough work? You bet!

A Dog's Body

A Coat of Many Colors: Most dogs have two coats of hair. The outer coat has long guard hairs to protect against the weather; the undercoat has short, fluffy hair to keep the dog warm. Most dogs shed their undercoat in the spring and grow it back in the winter.

Them Bones, Them Bones: Even though dogs come in drastically different sizes, they each have the same number of bones.

Tip to Toe: Dogs have 4 toes on each foot + an extra thumb-like toe called a *dewclaw* on each front foot. (Some dogs have dewclaws on their hind feet too.) Since dewclaws do not reach the ground, they serve no purpose and are often removed when the dog is still a puppy.

The Tooth of the Matter: Puppies have 32 temporary teeth. Adult dogs have 42 permanent teeth. The 12 small front teeth called *incisors* are used to pick up food. The 4 large, pointed *canine* teeth or *fangs* are used to tear meet. The 26 other *premolars* and *molars* are used to grind and crush food.

Ear, Ear!: A dog whose ears droop has *pendulous* ears. Some people *crop*, or cut, these to make short, stand-up ears. Some people also *dock* or cut off their dog's tail. Most people are

getting away from these practices. Dogs say thank goodness! Dogs have super hearing. They can hear very high-pitched sounds that people can't hear. They also hear over a longer distance. They can distinguish between very similar sounds. For example, a dog can tell the sound of your car's engine from that of another vehicle!

You Gotta Have Heart: A dog's heart beats 70-120 times a minute. Its normal body temperature is 101.5 degrees Fahrenheit. Dogs do not sweat. They cool their body by sticking out their tongue and panting. Evaporation of water from the mouth cools the dog's body.

The Nose Knows: A dog can smell odors millions of times too faint for a person to detect. A gland inside the dog's nose helps keep its nose wet. This moisture helps a dog's smelling ability. A dog will also lick its nose to help keep it moist.

See, See, Amigo: Dogs are color blind! They mostly see different shades of gray. They can't see patterns and forms as well as humans do, but their ability to see tiny movements makes them excellent hunters.

A Breed Apart

There are hundreds of breeds of purebred dogs in the world. A *purebred* dog has a father (sire) and mother (dam) who belong to the same breed. If a dog's parents belong to different breeds, it is a *crossbred*. A dog whose ancestors are from

many different breeds is called a *mongrel* or *mutt*.

The American Kennel Club is the main organization of dog breeders in the U. S. It registers 125 breeds of dogs in 6 groups:

Sporting dogs: 24 breeds of pointers, setters, retrievers and spaniels. Pointers and setters smell the air to find birds and then point their body toward it to guide the hunter. Retrievers pick up birds that have been shot and bring them back to the hunter. They can do this on land or water. Spaniels *spring* or scare birds from bushes into the air.

Hounds: 20 breeds hunt by smell or sight. Scent hounds like beagles and foxhounds run with their nose to the ground. Coonhounds *bay* or give long, deep barks while they trail game. Gazehounds or sight hounds are tall and slender and hunt by sight. Gazehounds like greyhounds and whippets are used in dog races. Other gazehounds include the Afghan hound and the saluki.

Working dogs: 32 breeds make up the largest breed group. Working dogs include collies, Shetland sheepdogs and Welsh corgis, which herd cattle and sheep. Doberman pinschers and German shepherds make good guard dogs. Alaskan malamutes, Samoyeds and Siberian huskies pull sleds.

Terriers: 23 breeds. Originally bred to drive game out of holes in the ground. Their name comes from *terra*, Latin for earth. Most terriers have a wiry coat and bushy beard. They are good watchdogs and like to kill mice, rats and snakes.

Toy dogs: 15 breeds, mostly pets. Poodles and Manchester terriers also belong to this group. Toy breeds come from all over the world. The Chihuahua was developed in Mexico. The Pekingese comes from China. The Papillon is from Spain. The

largest toy dog is the pug, which can weigh up to 18 pounds.

Non-sporting Dogs: 11 breeds, mostly pets. Originally bred for work or sport. Peeles once retrieved ducks for French hunters. Dalmatians have herded cattle and hunted game.

Draw a Picture!

Below (if this is your own book!), draw a picture of all the kinds of dogs you can think of. Examples: pet dogs, tired dogs (feet), iron dogs (that go in front of a fireplace), hot dogs (that you eat), etc.!

Around the World With Dogs

You just *think* your dog came from Ohio! But dog breeds began all over the world, and much longer ago than you might expect. See the list below. On a world atlas, locate the country the dog is from. Figure out how old the breed is.

DOG BREED	COUNTRY	YEAR
Chesapeake Bay Retriever	United States	1800
Irish Setter	Ireland	1700
Labrador Retriever	Newfoundland	1800
Pointer	Spain	1650
Basset Hound	France	1600
Beagle	England	1600
Dachshund	Germany	1700
Chihuahua	Mexico	1500
Pekingese	China	700
Alaskan Malamute	Alaska	1000 B. C.
Boxer	Germany	1800
Collie	Scotland	1600
Doberman Pinscher	Germany	1800
German Shepherd	Germany	1800
Old English Sheepdog	England	1800
Rottweiler	Germany	50 A. D.
Siberian Husky	Siberia	1000 B. C.
Schnauzer	Germany	1400
Boston Terrier	Boston, Massachusetts	1870
Bulldog	England	1200
Chow Chow	China	150 B. C.

©1997 Carole Marsh/Gallopade, 359 Milledge Ave., Atlanta, GA 30312/1-800-536-2GET/Page 16

Sex Ed, Dog Style

Adult dogs can mate anytime. Females mate only during *estrus* or "heat". This happens about every 6 months and lasts 3 weeks.

If you don't want your dog to have puppies, it is best to take them to the vet and have them *spayed* (female) or *castrated* (male). This does not hurt the dog.

So many unwanted dogs end up on the streets or in shelters where they are finally killed (to make room for more homeless dogs). Please don't add to this problem!

A mother dog carries her young 9 weeks (instead of 9 months for humans) before they are born. Most litters have 1-12 puppies (but at least 15 have been reported!).

Dogs are mammals. Mammals feed their young on milk from the mother's body. A mother dog nurses her pups for the first 6 weeks.

Puppies are born with their eyes closed and ears sealed. They both open 13-15 days after birth. Around 3 weeks, they start to walk. From 4-10 weeks, puppies form close relationships with their mother and littermates. A good time to adopt a puppy is when it's 6-8 weeks old.

Dogs are fully grown from 8 months-2 years. Large dogs grow slower than small dogs! A 6 month old puppy is the same (in development) as a 10-year-old kid; a 2 year-old-dog to a 24-yea-old adult. After that, each dog year = 4-5 human years. Most dogs live 12-15 years.

Bow Wow!: The Dog's Bark

By 4-weeks-old, a puppy can talk in barks, growls, howls, whines and yelps. Each sound is its way to communicate with you and with other dogs.

Dogs also communicate with "body language", their eyes and odors. That's why dogs urinate on trees -- to mark their territory.

Tombstone Territory

Dogs use *instinctive* behavior. This means it is inherited, not learned from training or experience. So, a dog may turn around several times before it lays down (just like a wild animal does to trample leaves or grass to make a bed).

A dog is also very defensive of its home turf or *territory*. Its *home range* (your neighborhood) is a neutral area and dogs agree to let each other go there.

I Love My Ohio Dog

Dog Food for Thought

Feed your dog a good quality commercial dog food. Table scraps should not make up more than 1/4 of your dog's diet.

Feed puppies small meals 4 times a day until they are 3 months old. From 3-6 months, feed them 3 times a day. Feed them 2 times a day from 6-12 months. After that, you can feed your dog just once a day. Of course they love extra snacks and treats too!

Always be sure your dog has clean, cool water. It's ok for your dog to eat grass. And it's good for them to exercise their teeth and gums on dog biscuits, rawhide strips, or a raw soupbone.

In the Dog House: An indoor dog needs a clean place to sleep with blankets. An outdoor dog needs a good, dry doghouse.

Bride & Groom: Brush your dog several times a week to keep its coat clean and to stimulate its skin. A long-haired dog may need a haircut in the summer. Don't give your dog a bath too often or you will dry out its skin. Bathe it in warm water with mild soap and be sure and rinse it well. Check your dog's teeth, ears and toenails.

Playtime: All dogs need regular exercise. Take indoor dogs on a walk twice a day. But don't wear out a puppy or an older dog with long trips, or walks in hot weather.

Dogs enjoy chewy toys that won't break.

Get down on all fours with your dog -- it will know it's time to play. If you pant with your dog, it will pant (laugh!) back!

A Vet, I'll Bet: Be sure you take a new puppy to the vet to get its shots. Diseases dogs can get include *canine distemper*, *hepatitis*, *leptospirosis* and *parvovirus*. You'll also want it to get a *rabies* shot.

Dogs can get worms too. *Heartworms* are especially bad for dogs. They can even kill them. Every state has heartworms. They are caused by mosquitoes and your dog will need to have medicine before, during and after the summer season to prevent heartworms.

Fleas and ticks also pester dogs. You can dust your dog and where it sleeps with flea powder, and a flea collar may also help.

Above all, do not let your dog run in the street or it might get hit by a car. Never leave your dog locked up in the car, because if it gets too hot, it may die!

Obedience School

The best time to train your dog is while it's still a puppy. Be kind and patient, but be a firm leader. In fact, one of the best ways to discipline your puppy is to act like its mother would, whether that's a gruff bark of "NO!", a tap on the snout, or a shake of the back of its neck.

Teach your dog to come when you call. It also needs to learn that NO means NO. But don't hit your dog to train it.

You'll want to housebreak your dog right away.

When your puppy is 8 weeks old, get it used to wearing a collar and leash. Give your dog "heel", "sit", "stay" and "down" lessons for 10 minutes twice each day. Only teach your dog one new thing at a time. After it masters that command, go on to the next.

When your dog does what you want it to, praise it, pet it and give it a food treat. If it does the wrong thing, firmly say "No". Be sure to say and do the same thing each time, so you won't confuse your dog.

Show Off!

There are dog shows all over the U. S., including in Ohio. Many are sponsored by the AKC (American Kennel Club).

Dogs are judged by their looks in a *bench show* (where dogs are shown on a bench).

In a *field trial*, sporting dogs and hounds are judged on endurance, ability to scent game, obedience to commands, how quickly they find birds a hunter has shot, returning birds without hurting them, and ability to track other animals.

Dog History

Dogs belong to the dog family, *Canidae*. Domestic dogs of all breeds are called *Canis familiaris*.

The dog developed from a weasel-like animal called *Miacis*. This animal lived 40 million years ago. (Since this is also the cat's ancestor, I guess cats and dogs are distant cousins -- but I don't think they know it!)

About 15 million years ago came *Tomarctus*, which looked like a wolf. From Tomarctus came dogs, wolves, coyotes, jackals and foxes. Today's dogs probably developed from small Asian wolves or

an animal like the Australian dingo.

The dog was the first animal to be *domesticated*. People started taming dogs more than 12,000 years ago. Their garbage dumps may have first attracted dogs to the camps of nomadic hunters and plant gatherers. Dogs decided it was easier to feed on the leftovers of humans than it was to hunt!

People valued the dogs since they kept the campsite clean and barked warnings when strangers or animals approached. Then, they discovered the dog's ability to guard or hunt. Dogs were an important part of early trade in the Middle East over 4,000 years ago.

The ancient Greeks raised large hunting dogs called *mastiffs*. The Romans kept dogs as pets, as well as to hunt and herd sheep. The ancient Chinese had watchdogs and hunting dogs.

In the Middle Ages, Europeans used hounds to hunt. In the 1500's, an English scholar named John Caius wrote a description of 16 breeds of English dogs, which included hounds, mastiffs, sheepdogs and terriers.

Most of the breeds we know today were in Europe by the 1800's. The first kennel clubs were also formed then.

American Indians developed their own breeds of dogs before Europeans brought their breeds of dog to the New World.

New dog breeds still come about, including the miniature dogs that are now popular pets.

Famous Dogs in History and Legend

Argos: Ulysses' hunting dog. He was the only creature to recognize the Greek hero when he returned home disguised as a beggar after 20 years of adventure!

Balto: An Eskimo dog that led a dog team that carried diphtheria serum 650 miles from Nenana to Nome, Alaska in a 1925 blizzard.

Barry: A St. Bernard that rescued 40 people lost in the snows of Switzerland's St. Bernard Pass around 1800.

Caesar: The pet terrier of King Edward VII of Great Britain. He walked ahead of kings and princes in his master's 1910 funeral procession.

Cerberus: The 3-headed dog of Greek mythology that guarded the gates to the underworld.

Greyfriar's Bobby: A Skye terrier that went with his Scotch master to Edinburgh every market day. In 1858, the man died, but the dog lived for 10 more years by his grave.

Igloo: Admiral Richard E. Byrd's pet fox terrier. The dog flew with Byrd on flights over the North and South poles.

Laika: The first space traveler, this Russian dog was sent up in a satellite in 1957.

Dog Talk

Raining Cats & Dogs: Used to be "raining dogs and polecats"!

Barking Up the Wrong Tree: To be trying the wrong thing; coondogs used to bark at the tree the coon wasn't trapped in by mistake.

In the Dog House: To be in trouble; on restriction

Dog Days: People used to believe dogs went mad in the hot summer.

Doggone Trivia

Dogs of War: Dogs have participated in many wars. Ancient Babylon troops used them. Spartans put spiked collars on them and send them against cavalry. Some dogs wore armor, like knights! Julius Caesar was met in Britain by fierce fighting dogs. King Henry VIII sent the King of Spain a pack of fighting dogs to use in the war against the French. The Germans trained German Shepherds for World War I. Belgian dogs pulled machine guns and even ambulances! The French had a dog messenger service. Dogs were used to find wounded soldiers in the American Civil War. In World War II, dogs patrolled for the enemy and gave "silent" warnings instead of barking. Dogs found mines and booby traps. Dogs even parachuted from airplanes! Today, police dogs fight another war -- the war against drugs by sniffing out hidden drugs.

City Dogs: Dogs help to keep our cities safe. Many work with police to guard businesses. Some are trained to scale walls, or even go through fire. Such a dog must be trained to track and catch a criminal, and yet be gentle with a lost child.

Winter Work Dogs: There are 3 types of Arctic dog: the Malamute is the strongest; the Samoyed is hardy; and the Husky has intelligence. These dogs are closely related to the

wolf and are covered in thick fur to protect them from severe cold.

Country Dogs: Country life and work would not be the same with out the dog. In the American West, the Border Collie is a favorite herd dog. The Welsh Corgi, used as a cattle dog, once worked as a butter wheel turner!

There are 3 types of gundogs. Spaniels flush birds or game out for the hunter. Pointers and setters "point" with their nose, tail and body, the direction of the game. Retrievers find the game and bring it back to its master. The first Labradors came to Britain with fishermen from northern Canada. The fishermen used the dog to retrieve seabirds they had shot from the boats. They trained the Labs to jump overboard and swim ashore with mooring ropes too!

Hunting hounds live in packs and may hunt fox or hares. Some track game by following a scent. Some watch for prey with their keen eyesight.

Terriers are also hunters. They were bred and trained to burrow and find small animals such as foxes, weasels and rats which could destroy crops.

Seeing-Eye Dogs: One of the most famous and popular kind of dog is one that helps blind people by being their "eyes". Seeing-eye dogs are trained at an early age so that they can become able companions to those without eyesight.

"Fire!": Dalmatians are often found at firehouses and speeding around on firetrucks heading to a fire.

Scooby Dooby Doo!: Read more about rare and unusual dogs such as the Chinese Crested, which is hairless except of a tuft of hair on top of its head; the Xoloitzcuintli (pronounced zow-low-eats-queen-tlee!) and called Xolo (zo-lo) for short; and the Shar-Pei, which seems to have twice as much skin as it needs!

Appendix

Great Pyrenees Club of Greater Pittsburgh
Carolyn Mohr
16473 Rock Creek Rd.
Thompson, OH 44086
(216)298-3489

Heart of Ohio Great Pyrenees Club
Pat Wallace
301 21st St. N.W.
Canton, OH 44709
(216)456-8496

Golden Retriever Club of Greater Toledo
Linda Copti
1023 Keeler St.
Maumee, OH 43537
(419)893-9833

***Siberian Husky Club of
Greater Cleveland, Inc.***
Patricia Mace
33800 Grafton Rd.
Valley City, OH 44280

Siberian Husky Club of Greater Canton, Inc.
Brenda Wise
3517 Sandy Lake Road
Ravenna, OH 44266

Trail Breakers Sled Dog Club
Karen Sundck
749 E. 343rd St.
Eastlake, OH 44094

Toledo Collie Club
Kathy Foley
5434 Armada Dr.
Toledo, OH 43623
(419)472-4638

Tri-State Rare Breed Club
(PA-VA-OH)
Jerry Bouslogh
111 S. Bon Air Ave.
Youngstown, OH 44509

Ohio Rare Breed Assn.
1711 Bank Place S.W.
Canton, OH 44706

American Tibetan Mastiff Assn.
Linda Steinnagel
P.O. Box 24312
Dayton, OH 45424-0312

Telomian Dog Club of America
Audrey Palumbo
28765 White Road
Perrysburg, OH 43551

Standard Schnauzer Club of America
Barbara Hendrix
105 Sheffield Road
Cincinnati, OH 45240
(513)771-4295

Keeshond Club of America
Ms. Jeanne Buente-Young
12440 Kiousville-Palestine Rd.
Mt. Sterling, OH 43143

The Working Border Collie
14933 Kirkwood Road
Sidney, OH 45365
(513)492-2215
$20/yr.

Borzoi International
33584 Overland Lane
Solon, OH 44139
$20/yr.($30/yr. foreign)

Cocker Spaniel Leader
Gene and Shirley Estel
9700 Jersey Mill Road N.W.
Pataskala, OH 43062-9750
(614)924-6004
$30/yr.($50/yr. foreign)

German Shorthaired Pointer News
Shirley and Cle Carlson
P.O. Box 850
St. Paris, OH 43072
(513)663-4773

Keeshonden
Keezette International
Keesette Inc.
Carol A. Cash
P.O. Box 81064
Cleveland, OH 44181

Buckeye Bull Terrier Club
Kayla Applebaum
2765 Som Cntr. Rd.
Huntington Valley, OH 44022
(216)464-0396

DVM
The Newsmagazine of Veterinary Medicine
Harcourt, Brace, Jovanovich, Publishers
7500 Old Oak Blvd.
Cleveland, OH 44130
$24/yr.

Support Dogs for the Handicapped
5900 N. High St.
Worthington, OH 43085

Man's Best Friend Award
National K-9
P.O. Box 30892
Columbus, OH 43230

Ohio State University-Columbus
College of Veterinary Medicine
1800 Cannon Drive
Columbus, OH 43210

Bearded Collie Club of America
Ms. Rosemary Schroeder
885 Gary's Lane
New Richmond, OH 45157

Basset Hound Club of America
Andrea Field
6060 Oak Hill Lane
Centerville, OH 45459

Little Lion Dog Club of America
Sandra Lunka
2771 Graylock Dr.
Willoughby Hills, OH 44094
(216)951-5288

Affenpinscher Club of America
Pat Dresser
1462 Granger Rd.
Medina, OH 44256

Guide Dogs for the Handicapped
(hearing ear dogs)
Jo Kiser
1178 Slade Ave.
Columbus, OH 43235
(614)451-2969

Hearing Dogs, Inc.
Cathy Nagaich
290 Hamilton Road N.
Gahanna, OH 43230
(614)763-4282(voice)
(614)471-7397(TTY)

Mobilization for Animals
(end animal suffering)
P.O. Box 1679
Columbus, OH 43216

Athens Search, Track & Rescue
Jon Tobin
75 E. State St.
Athens, OH 45701

Alaskan Malamute Club of America
Ione Zeller
8565 Hill Rd.
Pickerington, OH 43147

Bernese Mountain Dog Club of America
Becky Wolfert
115 Primrose Pl.
Lima, OH 45805

American Foxhound Club
Mrs. Jack H. Heck
1221 Oakwood Ave.
Dayton, OH 45419

English Setter Assn. of America
Mrs. Dawn Ronyak
114 S. Burlington Oval Dr.
Chardon, OH 44024

The Cesky Terrier Club of America
P.O. Box 178
Englewood, OH 45322

National Redbone Coonhound Assn.
Alys Kauble
Rt. 1 Box 142
Forest, OH 45843

Shiba Rescue and Info. Assn.
Mary Malone
8539 Schubert
Alliance, OH 44601

Irish Setter Club of Ohio
Nonda Jones
7578 River Road
Olmsted Falls, OH 44138
(216) 235-4197

Prestige Pet Products
9472-D Morrow Rossburg Road
Pleasant Plain, OH 45162

Canine Press (the newspaper for DogPeople!)
1147 Columbus Pike
Delaware, OH 43015
(614) 548-7649

101 Dalmations

Dalmations are especially popular in Ohio these days. Why? Because of the Walt Disney movie, many say!

Dalmations became very popular in Europe in the 19th century. They were used as carriage dogs. Dalmations are very good with horses and so they often accompanied carriages and guarded it and the horses while the owners were away.

Since the first fire "trucks" were really horse-drawn carriages, you'd find Dalmations on the scene there. Today, Dalmations are sometimes used for fire training.

Dog historians aren't really sure how Dalmations came to be. Some think they originated in Asia 300 years ago. You can find Dalmations in paintings and antique frescoes from Egypt and Greece.

But most people think the dogs began in the Middle East and traveled westward with bands of Gypsies to Yugoslavia, where they got their name from the town of Dalmatia.

The dogs were used as messengers during the Balkan Wars of 1912 and 1913. They have also been used as sled dogs, herd dogs and guard dogs.

All Dalmations are born completely white! They get their spots about 10 days later.

Animal Abusers Anonymous: 212-505-1073
Dial-A-Dog: 602-323-2275
Gaines Hotline: 800-842-4637
National Animal Poison Information Network: 217-333-3611
Search & Rescue Dogs: 800-727-2700

About the Author

Carole Marsh is a native of Marietta, Georgia. She is part Scotch-Irish and 1/16th Cherokee (her grandmother's name was Carrie Corn). The relative she most resembles was a former sea captain and lady's man who is said to have made -- and lost -- many a fortune.

The author has lived in a number of places, including the former port home of Blackbeard the Pirate. She is the author of more than 30 books about Ohio and has plans for many more. Her special focus is "strange things that are truer than fiction" and "truth-in-history".

She gets most of her ideas from students and teachers who ask to know "more about . . ." Currently, she is working on some true books about real-life werewolves and factual stories about alligators. She got interested in these two subjects when she learned about an actual werewolf that lived in the U. S. as recently as 1979 (and so could still be alive!) and when she found two 'gators taking a sunbath in her backyard.

Carole Marsh Ohio Books are produced for each day's orders in her "Book Bakery", so that the information is always as up-to-date as the day's headlines. Her daughter, Michele, runs the company, which likes to hear personally from teachers, librarians and readers.

Carole Marsh books are available in paperback, hardcover and on computer disk, and will soon be available on multi-media and CD-ROM formats.

You can write to the author in care of Gallopade Publishing Group. "I'd love to see clippings about true dog stories in your state!"

Glossary (Make a story with the words!)

Dog Days: Named by the Greeks. The hot, sticky days of late summer.

Dog Racing: Greyhounds race each other on an oval track. They chase a mechanical rabbit. The track is 1/4 mile long. Champion greyhounds can run more than 400 miles per hour. The dogs are put into starting box stalls like you see in a horse race. People bet on the dog they think will be the winner.

Dog Sled: A common transportation in Arctic regions. Made of wood with metal runners. Teams of 7-10 dogs pull the sleds over ice and snow. A team can haul more than 1,000 pounds. Sled dogs weigh from 50-100 pounds. They can pull a load twice their weight about 25 miles a day, going 2-5 miles an hour.

Dog Star: Sirius

Dogbane: Poisonous green plants that grow in the U. S. and Canada.

Dogear: The folded down page in a book.

Dogfight: Fight between combat planes.

Dogfish: Small sharks that have no bones. Lives in warm seas and grows to about 3 feet long. Some people eat dogfish. Its skin can be dried and used to polish wood.

Dogleg: To go one way, and then another; a bent golf course hole.

Dogtooth: A canine tooth (your eyetooth)

Dogtooth violet: A wildflower also called Adder's Tongue.

Dogwood: A beautiful tree that blooms white or pink blossoms.

Bibliography

The Ultimate Dog Book
by David Taylor, veterinary surgeon
A very attractive book just full of information about canines. Includes lots and lots of charming color photographs + info on choosing, training and caring for dogs -- even good old mutts. Teacher resource.
$29.95/Published by Simon & Schuster

What Kind of Dog Is That?: Rare & Unusual Breeds of Dogs
by Susan and Daniel Cohen
An interesting book about the more unusual breeds of dogs we see today and how they came to be. Good YA book!
$12.95/Published by Dutton

The Hound of the Baskervilles
by Arthur Conan Doyle
A creature made famous in a Sherlock Holmes story. The Hound was supposed to have had a strange luminescence and a fearful howl! Good Halloween treat?!

GOOD DOG CARL
by Alexandra Day
This and all the other "Carl" books are the most charming I've ever read. Well, you don't even have to read them -- there's only a word or two. The color artwork is charming and shows kids how to communicate without words. Great setting for a "Now, write your own story about what Carl is up to".

INDEX

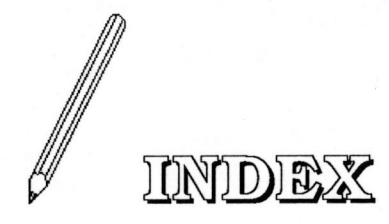

DOG:
Bark, 17
Behavior, 18
Body, 12
Bones, 12
Breeds, 10, 13
Care, 18-19
City, 23
Coat, 12
Country, 24
Drawing activity, 15
Eyes, 13
Famous, 21
Fire, 24
Food, 5, 11
Geography activity, 16
Hearing, 12
Heart, 13
History, 20-21
Math activity, 16
Nose, 13
Paws, 12
Rare, 24
Sayings, 22
Seeing-eye, 24
Sex ed, 17
Shows, 20
Stamp-licker, 10
Statistics, 11
Story to read aloud, 6
Teeth, 12
Training, 19
Trivia, 11, 23-24
War, 23